W9-AXU-719

SAFETY TOWN ®

Stop, Look, and Listen for Trains

By Dorothy Chlad

Illustrations by Lydia Halverson

CHILDRENS PRESS, CHICAGO

Library of Congress Cataloging in Publication Data

Chlad, Dorothy.
  Stop, look, and listen for trains.

  (Safety town)
  Summary: Greg briefly describes the types of cars
on freight and passenger trains and presents tips for
safety at railroad tracks and crossings
  1. Railroads—Juvenile literature. [1. Railroads—
Safety measures. 2. Safety] I. Halverson, Lydia, ill.
II. Title. III. Series: Chlad, Dorothy. Safety
town.
TF148.C49 1983   625.1′028′9   83-7213
ISBN O-516-O1988-O   AACR2

Hi. . . My name is Lyn.

I want to tell you about trains, railroad tracks, and railroad crossings.

ENGINE

CABOOSE

4

Every train has an engine. Some trains have a caboose, too.

Some trains are long. Some trains are short.

There are two kinds
of trains.
Some trains are
freight trains. Some
trains are passenger
trains.

FREIGHT TRAIN

PASSENGER TRAIN

TANK CARS

A freight train has
many kinds of cars.
Tank cars carry
liquids. . . milk, gasoline,
oil, or other things.

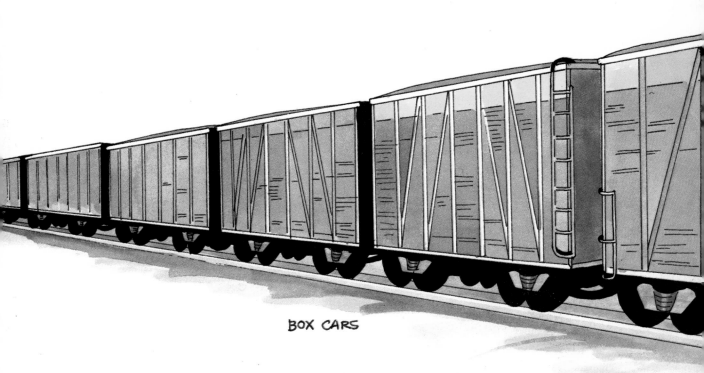

BOX CARS

Box cars carry
vegetables, meats,
furniture, or other
things.

FLAT CARS

Flat cars carry trucks,
cars, farm machinery,
lumber, or other things.

A passenger train has
three kinds of cars, too.
In the pullman car,
you can look out the
window and see things.

You can eat in the
diner car.

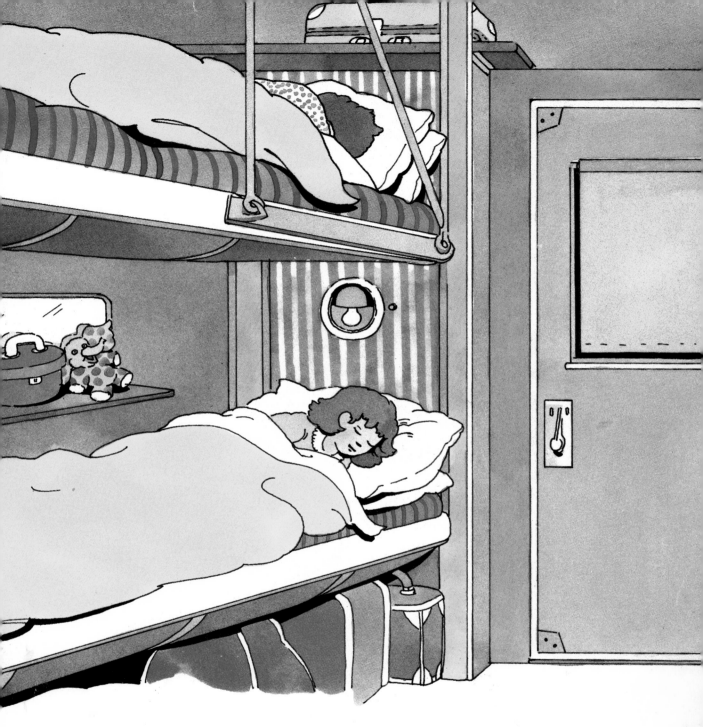

You can sleep in the
sleeper car.

It is fun to ride on trains. Trains take us to visit grandma and grandpa in the country... or to our friends in the city.

All trains go on railroad tracks. My friends and I never play on or near the railroad tracks.

17

Sometimes the tracks cross the street.

Before the train comes, lights blink and a whistle blows to let the people know a train is coming.

When a train comes,
cars, motorcycles, buses,
and trucks must stop.

Some railroad crossings
have gates that come
down. These gates tell
people that a train is
coming.

Trains go very fast.
My friends and I never
get close to the train
or railroad tracks.

We wait until the
train is gone. Then we
cross the tracks.

Drivers always stop,
look, and listen before
crossing the tracks.

When it rains or snows, it is very slippery. You must be very careful.

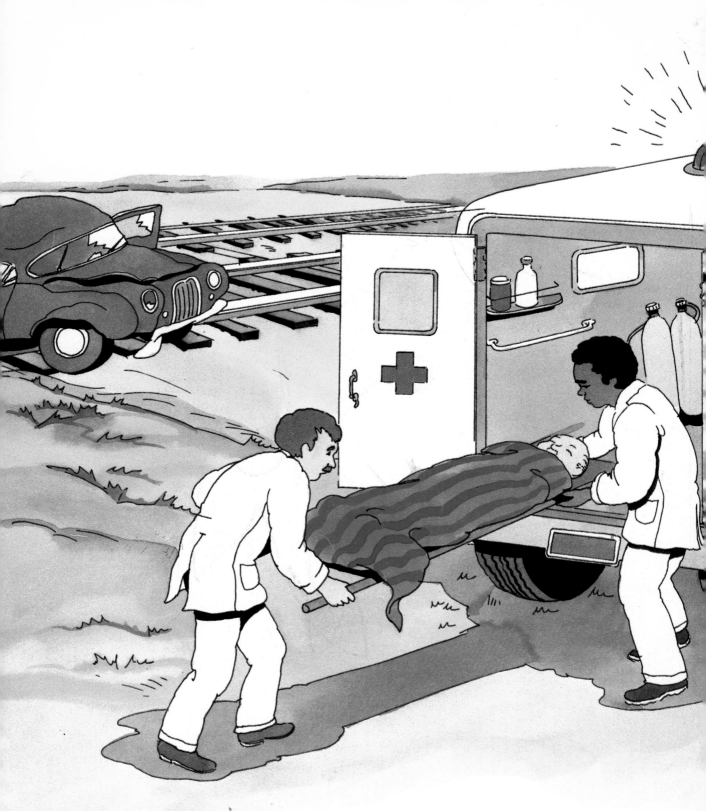

When people are
not careful, they can
have an accident and
get hurt.

My friends and I do
not want you to be hurt
so please remember our
safety rules.

1. Stop, look, and listen at railroad tracks.

2. Never play on or near the railroad tracks.

3. Wait until the train is gone before crossing the tracks.

About the Author

Dorothy Chlad, founder of the total concept of Safety Town, is recognized internationally as a leader in Preschool/Early Childhood Safety Education. She has authored six books on the program, and has conducted the only workshops dedicated to the concept. Under Mrs. Chlad's direction, the National Safety Town Center was founded; to promote the program through community involvement.

She has presented the importance of safety education at local, state, and national safety and education conferences, such as National Community Education Association, National Safety Council, and the American Driver and Traffic Safety Education Association. She serves as a member of several national committees, such as the Highway Traffic Safety Division and the Educational Resources Division of National Safety Council. Chlad was an active participant at the Sixth International Conference on Safety Education.

Dorothy Chlad continues to serve as a consultant for State Departments of Safety and Education. She has also consulted for the TV program "Sesame Street" and recently wrote this series of safety books for Childrens Press.

A participant of White House Conferences on safety, Dorothy Chlad has received numerous honors and awards including National Volunteer Activist and YMCA Career Woman of Achievement.

About the Artist

Lydia Halverson was born Lydia Geretti in midtown Manhattan. When she was two, her parents left New York and moved to Italy. Four years later her family returned to the United States and settled in the Chicago Area. Lydia attended the University of Illinois, graduating with a degree in fine arts. She worked as a graphic designer for many years before finally concentrating on book illustration.

Lydia lives with her husband and two cats in a suburb of Chicago and is active in several environmental organizations.